Tips for Successfully Passing the Real Estate Exam

And Generate Income in Your First 90 Days!

John D. Mayfield

DEDICATION

I dedicate this book to my lovely wife, Kerry. Thank you for always supporting and encouraging me.

CONTENTS

Introduction 1

Preparing for the Course 2

Studying and Preparing for the Exam 13

Exam Day 24

Finding the Right Company to Work For 34

How to Get Real Estate Leads to Generate Income 44
for Your Real Estate Career

About the Author 54

Think about a vacation you plan to take in the coming weeks, or perhaps, you are preparing for a special meal for your family. What would you begin to do before either of these events? Chances are, you would start to make a list of to-do's or tasks to make sure everything goes off without a hitch. Planning is crucial, and it helps to prepare you for the optimal or intended outcome.

You could say the same for a future road trip to a destination you may have never visited. Recently, I was speaking to a group in Kansas City. I was provided the location address by the group planner, but for me, this was a new area — not to mention an address that was also foreign to me. Luckily, I was able to put the street address into my car's GPS, and the GPS guided me directly to the job site.

Tips for Successfully Passing the Real Estate Exam and Generate Income in Your First 90 Days is a guide to help you prepare for your new adventure as a future real estate professional. It's your GPS to help lead you to a destination of opportunity and freedom — a guide to providing the first steps to becoming your "own boss" in a career that I have cherished for over 41 years, since the age of 18.

Each day you can study a new tip to not only help you prepare for the real estate course and exam but, more importantly, teach you how to generate income during your first 90 days as a real estate professional.

Enjoy the book and best of luck with pursuing your new career in the real estate field.

Preparing for the Course

Getting Ready to Take the Real Estate Course

Tip #1: Set a timeline to complete the school.

"Mom, I have a research paper due tomorrow. Can you help me?" Sound familiar? If not, perhaps you are one of the more detailed, organized, planning types of individuals, and this problem never darkened your school days. Unfortunately, for most of us, putting off our assignments until the last day was a significant part of our school study process. Using this procedure to prepare for the real estate exam is not a good tactic. And let's face it — for many of you, it may be your first trip back to school in many years. If so, why not get your new educational adventure off to a good start?

The best way to approach going back to (real estate) school is to set a definite timeline on when you plan to finish the course. At the Global Real Estate School, students have 90 to 120 days (dependent upon your state) to complete our coursework. I realize this period may sound short to some people; however, why extend the course out any longer? If you want to get your real estate license, then do it! Don't procrastinate. Sign up, go to school, and set a timeframe for finishing the coursework. I even encourage you to set a suggested date on when you plan to sit for the examination.

What is a reasonable timeframe to sign up for school and plan to finish? It depends on whether you plan to attend a live school or an online course. For live (in-person) schools, you know up front when your course will end. However, many students find an in-person course challenging and too demanding to attend with work, home, and life commitments.

In our online course, most students at the Global Real Estate School will finish within four to five weeks. Some students will complete as soon as 20 to 21 days.

My philosophy is to get in and out of the course quickly. Three to four weeks is a good target; however, if you feel this is too fast for you, then readjust or set your target goal for five to six or seven weeks. The bottom line is that you need to set a timeline to complete the school and sit for the examination.

Tip #2: Get a dedicated notebook and comfortable writing instruments (pens or pencils) to take notes.

Remember when you made the trip to purchase supplies for your children before school started? Make a trip to buy supplies for your own school experience. I suggest you consider purchasing a dedicated notebook, one or two comfortable writing instruments, a calculator (discussed later in this section), and plain index cards.

Many students tell me that they prefer to highlight a book or paper document versus handwriting notes. I always suggest students take handwritten notes whenever possible. Avoid your computer or iPad if possible for note-taking. It only makes sense that having technology too close can be distracting. Unfortunately, you might find yourself checking email, looking at social media, news feeds, etc. Keep your mobile phone off, and use a pen (or pencil) for taking notes in a dedicated notebook.

In a recent article from Psychology in Action (July 8th, 2018), author Lucy Cui discusses the myth of highlighting as a study aid for performing better on exams. From Cui's research on several studies about this topic, her final verdict is as follows: "Highlighting text is not an effective or reliable way to study for a test. It may help if it's done effectively, which is often difficult for students but not by much. It could even hurt your ability to make inferences about the text." [1]

Does this mean you should avoid highlighting all together? Not at all. However, I do encourage you to take handwritten notes as you go through the course. Yes, you can go back through and highlight your handwritten notes, but during the session, write your notes to help you review and study later.

One important note on this topic: Find a writing instrument that you enjoy writing with and does not hurt your fingers. If you prefer a pencil over a pen, by all means, use a pencil. If you're a pen person, find the type of pen you write best with and that feels comfortable in your hand and then use this as your primary writing tool. Also, be sure to have a few extra pens on hand as you progress through the school.

Having the proper writing instrument and a dedicated notebook for note-taking is essential to get the most out of your real estate course.

Tip #3: Devote a quiet place to study.

I remember back when I was 14 years old, and my mother began her studies and preparations for a career in real estate. One of her main items of concern was where she would go in our home to study for the exam. My father set up a makeshift desk using a card table in a separate part of our house where she would go after she finished her class time. This area was my mother's quiet place to read, take practice exam questions, and much more.

Several years later, my wife started a real estate school to help me with my real estate office. We also used a dedicated room upstairs in our home where she could go to be by herself to prepare and study for the real estate exam. Like my mother's success from this tip, it also worked for my wife!

Yes, you must find a place in your home where you can be free from distractions and noises. Find an area where you can focus on the material to get the maximum amount of studying done as possible. If you are not fortunate to find a private, quiet spot in your home, then, by all means, use your local public library. My local library has an excellent environment for studying, including several private glassed rooms for those needing an even quieter setting.

Some of you might be okay with a little background noise and prefer a coffee shop environment. You need to get in the habit of going to that special place where you can maximize your study potential outside of the classroom.

Tip #4: Dedicate a specific time each day to study and actually do it.

Check the following that applies to your study preference:

The "best" time of the day for me to study for the real estate course would be:

□ Early morning before I go to work

□ Mid to late morning after everyone leaves the house

□ Afternoon before dinner

□ After work/dinner, early evening, and before retiring for bed

Although this tip could easily fall in our next section of the tips book, making a commitment before beginning the course is the right decision for you to follow through. There is no right or wrong method with this tip, except that you do need to devote a portion of each day to preparing and studying for the real estate exam.

Whatever you choose, commit to that time slot from the start of your real estate school until the end. Be faithful to your decision and set aside a specific time to allot to studying your course materials.

One last word about the time of day you decide to study for the exam: It's okay (and recommended) to have more than one time slot devoted to studying. For example, use the early morning to review flashcards and past material.

Apply the evening after work to go through new information. If you are a full-time student, choose the morning for review and the afternoon for new material or vice versa.

Tip #5 - Get a good, bigger-sized calculator to use during school and for the exam.

Okay, first things first — don't panic, worry, fret, or give up on a career in real estate just because you have heard there is a lot of math on the test. The reality is that yes, there is math on the exam. However, the good news is, the math is not complicated. If you can multiply, divide, add, and subtract, you will be just fine.

Most pre-license real estate schools will have easy-to-learn methods for solving math problems. Global Real Estate School offers many math solutions from our YouTube channel to help you with your math studies. Go to YouTube and search for Global Real Estate School for more information.

If you want to attack the math problems with a vengeance and make this a non-issue for your real estate school days, get yourself the right calculator! Make sure it is a basic calculator, with functions to add, subtract, divide, etc. You cannot bring a financial or programmable calculator into the test center. Just look for something basic and BIG!

It's important that from day one of your real estate studies, you use the same calculator you will use on the test date. Becoming familiar with the keys and display on your calculator is essential. I keep stressing the word "big," but you must have something you can easily read and press the correct keys, more importantly. Many of the math problems are what I call freebies. If you miss one of these straightforward questions due to an error in pressing an incorrect key or reading the display wrong, is not good when tallying the final results.

Trust me, in my 30+ years of teaching pre-license real estate courses, I have witnessed many students bring some of the smallest calculators to class. Many are almost comical, especially when they have to use the eraser portion of their pencil to press the numeric keys to perform the calculations. In every case, I encourage the students to throw that calculator as far away from your studies as possible and invest in a reasonable $5 to $10 big, basic calculator. Again, nothing fancy, just a calculator to perform essential math functions.

Finally, remember that you cannot take mobile phone devices into the exam room, so don't use your mobile phone to practice during the real estate school. Get in the habit of using the same calculator you plan to use on your test day from day one of your real estate school program. Remember, your real estate school is your dress rehearsal for the big performance (exam day). Begin by preparing from day one with the right props — a basic, large calculator you will use on your opening performance (exam day), so you will pass your exam on the first attempt. (One final note, some testing centers may require you to use their calculators. If so, don't panic, you will do just fine).

Tip #6 - Sign a pledge card to yourself before you begin your real estate school.

Example: My Pledge and Commitment

I, _____, do herby pledge and commit that I will avoid the following activities during my real estate school enrollment. I will continue to avoid and refrain from the following until after I pass my real estate examination.

- I will NOT spend time watching TV. Instead, I will devote my time to my real estate course and study the course material.
- I will AVOID social media and stay off of my computer, except to take my real estate course and review for the exam.
- I will LIMIT my use of email and web surfing until AFTER I complete my real estate school and pass the real estate exam.
- I will NOT read outside material, books, magazines, newsletters, etc., until AFTER I complete my real estate school and pass the real estate exam.
- I commit to use the next 30 to 60 days and devote this time to studying and preparing to pass my real estate exam. I will use my free time to review, complete, or prepare for the real estate exam so that I can pass the examination on the first attempt.
- I will state the following affirmation daily up to and until I pass my real estate examination on the first attempt.

I am a great real estate school student, and I am learning the material for the real estate examination with ease. I will pass the real estate exam on my first attempt!

_____   _____

Name   Date

[1]   https://www.psychologyinaction.org/psychology-in-action-1/2018/1/8/mythbusters-highlighting-helps-me-study

Study and Preparing for the Exam:

Tips on How to Study to Pass the Exam

Tip #1: Commit to daily study.

If you want to have success with your real estate studies, then you MUST commit to studying every day! Unfortunately, I see many students who study a few days here and there. They study one day and take one or two days off. You cannot follow this plan because this type of studying will not work.

Think about the athlete who is preparing for the big game or the individual who wants to lose weight. Practicing only a few days a week or eating unhealthy foods every other day will not provide you with the needed efforts to win the game or lose the weight. If you plan to succeed at whatever challenge you face, you must put in disciplined effort and study daily.

As with tip #4 from the previous section, committing to studying the real estate material every day is essential if you want to pass the real estate exam.

Tip #2: Make flashcards.

Understanding the definitions is a BIG part of passing the real estate exam. In some ways, attending real estate school is a lot like learning a new language. At Global Real Estate School, we offer a unique opportunity to download real estate definitions (digital flashcards) right to your mobile phone! Go to www.globalrealestateschool.com and look for our digital flashcard offer. The digital flashcards are easy to download and effective at helping you learn the terminology to pass the real estate exam. Having your digital flashcards available on your phone provides you the opportunity to study whenever you find yourself with a few extra minutes.

If you prefer to make your flashcards, write the definition on one side of a 3 x 5 index card and the description on the flip side.

Flashcards will help you learn the definitions of real estate terminology, and knowing the explanations will help you pass the exam on your first attempt!

Tip #3: Carve out additional study time — listen to Global Real Estate School's podcast, review the digital flashcards, or the cards you prepared, but study during other times you might not have considered reviewing the material.

Now the critical part, USE your flashcards! Yes, take them with you wherever you go and review your cards when you have any free time. Unfortunately, I have witnessed many students take the time to create flashcards, take excellent notes in class, but fail to carve out the additional time to review and study.

Whether you plan to attend a live pre-license real estate school or an online course, you must carve out a time slot during the day or evening to study. Otherwise, you could very easily forget the information after a few days. Reviewing every day will help you remember and retain for your big test day.

Tip #4: Practice reading the information two or three times.

A friend of mine who is an excellent real estate broker often reminds students to read the exam questions a minimum of three times — once for you, once for your broker and once for the exam. His words of wisdom do help while taking the test. Yes, I will also include this tip in your next section. Why? Because I want to stress how valuable this advice is for you as a real estate school student. By practicing this concept now and on exam day, it will become second nature for you to repeat.

Unfortunately, many of the exam questions are designed to trip students up and to force you to pick the wrong answer. However, the good news is that you don't have to answer the so-called trick questions incorrectly when you take the test. If you choose to build the habit of reading the questions or information two or three times, you will do great on exam day.

Just remember, reading the question once may not truly open your eyes to what the exam writer is asking, but reading the question two or three times does something magical. The best choice will always rise to the top.

Tip #5: Take as many practice exams as possible.

I realize many students get tired of taking practice exams. However, you need to answer as many practice questions before the exam day as possible. There are many reasons why reading and repeating these in advance of your test is beneficial. First, you will probably see similar questions on the exam, which no doubt will help you earn a passing grade. Second, you will get your body and mind in shape for when the big day arrives.

Using the athlete analogy once more, you must prepare for the exam as if it is the BIG game. Without any preparation or practice, the two-and-a-half hours of exam questions will wear you down quickly. On the flip side, practicing as many times as possible will prepare you for your test, both mentally and physically.

At Global Real Estate School, we have an excellent test preparation package you can purchase with 500+ multiple-choice exam questions. Best of all, our questions are all national content, so regardless of the state you live in, these questions will help you for the exam in your state. For additional information, go to www.globalrealestateschool.com.

Tip #6: Watch other real estate instructors' approaches to math on YouTube.

Some instructors might disagree with me on this next tip. However, I am not one who tries to convince you that my way is the only method that works for all real estate school students. I think you should see if you can find someone who explains the math in an easy-to-follow way. Many instructors are putting their content on YouTube and other sites on the Internet. You could easily find someone who explains math problems better than your current teacher or me.

Just go to YouTube and search for real estate math or math problems for the real estate exam. You will find several instructors to choose from. Hopefully, you will find the right instructor who can give you another viewpoint and method for solving your math problems.

Tip #7: Avoid listening to outside sources, especially other real estate agents.

Although your friends and family members may mean well by trying to give advice, be cautious. In my opinion, it is best to remain focused and only use the information and advice from your school instructors.

Unfortunately, there may be real estate agents in your office — even a friend or close acquaintance — who want to offer advice. Be careful! Remember, the exam changes regularly, and your school and instructors will have the latest information. They will know what is most beneficial for you to study to pass the exam.

Yes, you may be able to find a wealth of information online from other instructors and information regarding the real estate course. Be cautious and make sure the people you do listen to are actively teaching real estate courses.

At Global Real Estate School, we provide weekly (sometimes two or three times a week) classes through our YouTube channel and Global Real Estate School. You can also follow us on Instagram and like our Facebook page. Just search for Global Real Estate School. We provide a wealth of information that can help you in studying and preparing for the real estate exam.

Tip #8: Use positive affirmations.

Proverbs 18:21 reminds everyone that "death and life are in the power of the tongue." The words you speak are powerful and speaking positive words that you <u>will</u> pass the exam on your first attempt is important. Remind yourself daily that you learn the material easily, you are retaining the information you are studying, and on exam day, you will remember the information and answer all the questions correctly. Continue your affirmations with this statement, "I will pass the real estate exam on my first attempt and will become a successful real estate agent!"

Tip #9: No TV, no books, no social media — commit to staying laser-focused on your real estate studies.

Finally, the final tip for this section is a repeat from the previous section. Still, it is so vital that it's worth covering again. You have to refrain from watching TV, surfing the Internet, checking social media, or reading anything other than your study material. These activities can take up a lot of your time. Remember that your real estate school will only consist of three, four, or maybe five weeks of the most. It's so essential for you to use this time to devote yourself 100% to the real estate examination. Look at as a short-term sacrifice for a long-term investment. For many students, this career is satisfying and represents a financial advantage to themselves and their families. You can accomplish this goal by remaining focused on your real estate studies.

After all, this is a profession that you desire to be in; otherwise, you would not be reading this book, and you definitely would not be this far into the text. Recently, I happened to read about one of my former students (just a couple of months ago), who was at a closing with her buyers. For me, this is the joyous side of teaching this course — to see a former student celebrating and earning a commission check. She also reported several new listings in her Facebook posts.

I know it's tempting to want to take a break and relax your mind from real estate terminology. But if you must do so, take a walk or do something light and productive. That will not suck valuable time that could be devoted to your real estate studies. You have to commit and stay focused. Remember, no TV, no social media, no reading, and avoid other activities that will rob you from precious quality real estate studying time.

Exam Day:

Tips to Apply on the Big Test Day!

Tip #1: Stay relaxed; you got this! Repeat your affirmations.

Remain calm and relaxed before the examination. Repeat the affirmations that you memorized in the previous tips section. After all, you have studied and prepared for this big day, and you are more than ready to conquer the exam on your first attempt.

It is much easier to remain a coach on the sidelines and give advice or to tell someone not to worry; however, you have to find some way to keep your nerves and excitement from getting the best of you on exam day. Listen to some relaxing music on your way to the test site and repeat the words, I have studied hard. I know the information, and all of my answers needed for this exam will be available from my recall and retention. I am going to pass this exam today. On my first attempt!

Tip #2: Don't let early finishers bother you. (Note about other test takers)

Recently, I was allowed the opportunity to take the exam for another state to satisfy the requirements for becoming a school owner and licensed instructor. One interesting fact I discovered is that many of the students in the same exam room as you are not taking the real estate examination. Keep in mind as this could change from state to state. I was the only person at my testing agency taking their real estate examination. I mention this because one lady sitting next to me was taking her barber examination, which was only 50 questions. My test was 150 questions. Naturally, she finished the exam well before I did. Others might only be coming back to take a portion of the exam because they did not pass.

What you need to remind yourself of is that not everyone in the room will be taking the same length of examination that you are. If you see others get up and leave, don't take this as a sign that something is wrong with you. Stay focused and don't let the distractions of the early finishers disrupt your concentration.

Tip #3: Don't try to cram or study too hard.

As I've mentioned previously, if you followed all of the tips throughout this book, you are more than ready for today's exam. Do not try to cram or study too hard the night before or even the day of the test. I realize some people still like to follow this regimen. However, if you do plan to study, by all means, briefly go over some of the topics that you may still feel uncertain about. At globalrealestateschool.com, under the blog section, you can search for my webinar about the day before the exam preparation. During this short webinar, I quickly cover some of the main topics that would be good to know for the exam.

Again, use your judgment for this tip; however, too much studying the night before is not a good practice for passing the exam — especially staying up late trying to memorize or go over the material. Get a good night's rest and lightly study versus trying to pull an all-nighter going over the content.

Tip #4: Read each question and the possible answers three times before selecting your answer.

Read it once for yourself, a second time for the instructor who taught you the material, and a third time for the testing agency. Remember the tip provided earlier — start practicing this during your course studies. Many questions can trip you up simply because you didn't read the words correctly. On exam day, remind yourself to read each question two to three times, as well as each answer. Eliminate the answers that provide solutions that don't fit the scenario. As you reread the question two or three times, the correct answer may very well jump out at you. If not, I'm going to give you a secret tip in our next strategy on how to correctly answer any question that you may be having trouble with.

Tip #5: Eliminate the answers to the two best choices. If you do not know the answer, skip the question and return to it later.

Okay, so you've read the question and each possible answer two to three times and you still are uncertain of the correct answer. Here's the secret tip: Skip the question and come back to it later. Often, you will find another item somewhere down the road in the exam that will help you answer the question you are stumped on. Leave your choices blank until you're ready to answer because you can always come back to them later and give them another try.

Again, don't panic or become anxious just because you may find two or three questions that you cannot answer. There's a good chance you'll discover the answers as you continue through the course.

Tip #6: Don't overthink the questions or add information to the question.

This is one of the most significant pieces of advice I can provide any test taker. Students will often ask me about a problem, and I will provide the answer. The same students will then want to insert what-ifs or what-abouts or couldn't-this-also-happen into the problem. Any time you begin to add more information into the question, you're going to get yourself in trouble. Read the question you have to answer the exact way that it's worded. If you find yourself overthinking or adding unnecessary information not provided in the original question, stop!

If you follow this process, you will pass the real estate exam on your first attempt.

Tip #7: Don't change your answers!

My second most significant piece of advice I can provide to test-takers is not to change your answers! There is a caveat for this — if you recognize some mistake you made in reading the first question or performing in math calculation, don't hesitate to change your answer. Otherwise, if you are stumped and don't have a gut feeling about providing a specific choice, revisit tip #5. When you return to the question, make an educated guess if the answer still isn't obvious and stick with that decision. Do not make a change or switch answers.

You've been studying diligently for the last few weeks, and there's lots of information that has been processed and stored deep in your subconscious mind. Often, those answers are creeping their way back to provide you clues and extra information. When you see a question and you are unsure of the answer, you may have a gut feeling telling you to go with answer C, which is correct 99.9% of the time. Why? Again, it's your subconscious reminding you of the information that it has stored for that topic. Go with your gut feeling and don't change your answers.

Tip #8: Double-check all math problems. Work through them backward to make sure they work.

This response probably sounds relatively simple and straightforward. However, a lot of students will bypass the suggestion and miss 3–4 questions due to silly mistakes. Therefore, double- and triple-check your math calculations!

Writers love to write questions in such a way that the student might miss it by failing to read each word carefully. Math problems will sometimes use the terms quarterly or semiannually, so you have to ensure you convert these correctly to solve the problem. In other words, if they want a quarterly figure, they may word the question in a tricky way that implies they want an annual answer, but really want you to figure out the quarterly number. They will give you the annual figure as answer (a) and the quarterly figure as answer (b). You may instinctively want to choose answer (a), therefore bypassing the last step, which is to divide by four.

Exam writers will try to figure out the most common mistakes students make on math problems and include those answers with the problem. If you do not double- or triple-check the math solutions, you may have made the obvious mistake and selected the wrong choice.

Take your time. Double-check your math, and you will be just fine!

Tip #9: Make sure you have not left any questions unanswered.

Never leave any questions blank, and go with your gut feeling if you're still uncertain about a question. Your subconscious is a good note taker and can provide excellent help on your exam day. After all, you have a 25% chance of getting something right by selecting a choice versus leaving something blank.

Most computerized tests will warn you that there are choices left blank, and some may only allow you to finish the test by having every answer marked. However, it never hurts to double-check that you answered all of the questions before exiting your exam.

Tip #10. Congratulations!

You're finally done, and all you have left is to click the exit button and finish up your evaluation for the testing agency. You move toward the exit door to retrieve your personal belongings and discover your results. I want to be the first one to say congratulations. I knew you could pass the exam on your first attempt!

I genuinely believe that following the tips provided for you will help you pass the exam on the first attempt and move you one step closer to your new career as a real estate professional. In the next section, I want to help you find the right real estate broker in your new role as a real estate professional. Then, I will conclude by giving you some tips on how to generate income in your first 90 days. Again, congratulations on passing the real estate exam! I knew you could do it.

Finding the Right Company

to Work For

Tip #1: Make a list of what you would like to ask brokers and what you hope to find in your agency.

Congratulations on passing your real estate exam. Now it's time to find the right real estate agency to work for. It's always a good idea to think about the traits and qualities you hope your new broker/manager will possess. In fact, it may be useful for you to make a list of managers you have worked for in the past and leaders you respect and admire and the qualities you appreciated about them. It may also be useful to list the traits that you wished your leader had possessed or how you wished they had managed you differently. Performing this exercise will enable you to discover some of the important qualities that you hope to find in your new broker/manager.

After all, there are many different leadership styles, and you want to make certain that you're gravitating toward a style that you have enjoyed working for in the past.

Tip #2: List the potential brokers in your area.

Remind yourself that it is important to speak to more than one real estate broker during the interview process. It's true — many real estate brokers will try to sweep you off your feet during the first meeting but understand there may be a better fit for you with another broker across town.

Through my 41 years of experience as a real estate broker and as someone who has taught pre-license real estate school since 1987, finding the right agency is a critical step in your career. I have witnessed many real estate agents choose the wrong broker, which ultimately led to the end of their real estate career. You want to find someone who is going to provide education, training, encouragement, and the resources and environment that will help you grow your real estate business.

By making a list of the agencies in your area and the size of the organizations, you can begin to make appointments with three or four different brokers.

Tip #3: Talk to your friends and other agents for suggestions and advice.

Now that you have a list of the brokers in your area and perhaps a possible list of those you'd like to visit, I encourage you to talk to some of your friends, coworkers, family, and close acquaintances as to who they might suggest you talk to from your list. Many will have experiences from buying or selling real estate and will be able to provide feedback on the quality of the service from the individual help, as well as the company. Try to narrow your focus to three or four appointments.

Tip #4: Research the brokers' websites, advertisements, and more.

It is a good idea to visit the brokers' websites with whom you have appointments. Find out if their website is up-to-date, looks user-friendly, and promotes the real estate agents working for their organization.

Check to see if the website offers a spotlight for the agents. Do the agents have photos on the website? You can usually discover this feature if you click on an agent's name, then drill down to another page on the website. Once on this page, look to see if there are videos or interesting information under the 'About Us' or 'About the Broker' page. You definitely want to look at each one of these brokers you've researched and discover how appealing their website is and how it may be perceived by consumers.

If you've narrowed down your list to two or three brokers and their websites look unprofessional or out-of-date, then you probably need to look for other brokers to interview. The Internet is such a critical part of marketing in today's world that it's essential you work for a broker or manager who has a website to attract potential buyers and sellers!

As a side note, it's okay to do some social media stalking of these brokers and managers, too. Look them up on Facebook, Twitter, Instagram, or even YouTube, and see how active they are. Try to discover if there are any differences or issues you may not approve of. In fact, I'm thinking about hiring a coach for my own speaking and training business. One potential candidate posted some very derogatory information last night on her Instagram account. She gave me such a bad feeling that there is no way I would use her as a coach. You may see some of the same information about a broker or manager you're getting ready to interview with and how they use social media. These are red flags, and needless to say, this would not be a very pleasant environment for you to work in. You don't want to think about having to change offices quickly.

Tip #5: Make a list of questions before meeting with your brokers you have selected.

Questions you might consider asking are, what training and education do you provide? What is your initial commission or compensation, split, and more importantly, can that commission compensation increase over time? In other words, the more you produce, the more you should be able to earn. You also want to ask questions about floor time. How are incoming lead calls handled? Do you get a website? Are there any expenses that are paid by the company (postage, advertisements, etc.). Are there company bonuses, prizes, or gifts/contests where you can generate income or special trips and vacations?

Also, ask if the broker is involved with the local Association of REALTORS®. For me, this is a huge opportunity to discover whether he or she is in tune with today's real estate industry. Granted, not all brokers have time to attend local, state, or national REALTOR® meetings; however, those who do participate show interest in the organization.

I think it's also essential to find out what the initial joining fees are. Is the broker a member of the local Association of REALTORS®, MLS? Will they assist with paying for or refunding dues you may have to pay? Find out how often the brokerage provides sales meetings. Also, do they have a mentorship program? Ask them about the company and if it has a social media presence. For example, do they have a Facebook page or Instagram account? Is the account updated regularly?

Are there photographers in the office? Do they have someone who will assist you with paperwork and other activities as you generate business? Are there desk fees or additional incidental costs you may incur?

You want to have some questions prepared to be sure the broker will be a good fit for you. Develop a list of questions and make sure that you're comfortable asking them before going in for your interview.

Tip #6: Talk to other Agents in the Company, but always more than one or two.

I encourage you to talk to other agents in the company, if possible — more than one or two agents would be ideal. Ask them how happy they are working for the organization and perhaps see if they can provide feedback or suggestions that might help you before choosing this broker.

Also, it would be a good idea to find out if there are any quirks or problems that might be going on inside the organization. This can be a severe issue. You would regret choosing an organization where there might be three to four (or more) individuals preparing to exit due to problems in the company.

If you're in a small- to medium-sized market, you could even go to the local Association and ask if there's a lot of agent turnover for specific real estate brokerages in the area. Most local REALTOR associations would provide this information, especially in general terms. However, I actively discourage you from asking questions about a specific broker. There's nothing wrong with asking if turnover is high at one particular real estate company.

Tip #7: It's okay to go back for a second time.

Remember, it's okay to go back for a second interview. You might get a different impression on the second visit, as there may be different people working in the office. You could even ask the broker after your initial interview if it would be okay for you to come back for a second visit.

You've done your homework, and now you're ready to complete your application paperwork so that you can begin your career as a real estate professional. In the next chapter, we're going to look at some tips and suggestions on how you can start generating income during your first 90 days as a real estate professional.

How to Get Real Estate Leads to Generate Income for Your Real Estate Career

Tip #1: Build a Database

If you want true success as a real estate professional, then you must build a good database of your friends, family members, and coworkers (past and present). Your database is essential, but it can even go beyond just your sphere of influence. My good friend and successful real estate broker and coach Darren Kittleson says that you must have a "met" database. Yes, when you meet someone, send them a card and add them to your database!

Every year, the National Association of REALTORS® publishes an extensive study titled, "Profile of Homebuyers and Sellers." I have followed and read this study carefully every year. One interesting question they almost always ask consumers is, "How did you find your real estate agent?" Overwhelmingly, year after year, the consistent finding is that a recommendation from a friend, family member, or coworker is the category with the highest percentage!

Think about this answer: Anytime someone refers you to a potential real estate lead, half your work is already done for you. In fact, if someone gives you a referral for yard work, remodeling, plumbing, an automobile salesperson, a doctor, etc., what do you usually do with this referral? You end up using their services! Why? Because your friend had a good experience and trusted the person or product, and this made you feel more comfortable purchasing or buying the same commodity or service. If your friend recommends this person, then they must be good.

Remember, if you want to build a successful real estate business, you must create a good database! At Global Real Estate School, we offer a 60 Days to Success real estate program. The program walks you through the proper steps for building a database that will provide you the results needed to generate income during your first 90 days as a real estate professional.

Tip #2: Send Out a Press Release to the Local Media

I read an exciting book several years ago on the topic of public relations, and one interesting fact jumped out at me in the book. The author (a public relations and newspaper editor) reminded the readers that while news outlets are hungry for information to help fill a newspaper, radio program, news story, and more, news editors and television and radio personalities have lives too. They want to enjoy time with their families, eat dinner at regular times, and more. They may even be searching for a new home or know someone who is — yet another referral! Depending on the size of your community, this tip is a no brainer. Best of all, it's FREE!

I've prepared a sample press release you can use at globalrealestateschool.com under our resources tab. Look for your FREE press release template in the New Agent Toolkit.

Tip #3: Take Advantage of Social Media

Another FREE source is social media. I understand not everyone likes Facebook, Instagram, and Twitter (and yes, we could go on and on). However, social media is still a BIG medium to use to get your message out to the masses. And best of all, it's FREE!

Granted, you can pay for social media ads and target specific consumers in your market area, but for the most part, use your database you created under the first tip in this section. Next, connect and network with your list through social media platforms like Facebook, LinkedIn, and others.

Once you make connections, it is important that you regularly stay in touch and network appropriately. Make sure your comments and likes are genuine. Set aside limited time each day to see what your connections are posting. You will learn a wealth of information about your database and will be able to use social media as an excellent tool for touching your sphere of influence. Best of all, your connections will be able to follow you and your new journey as a real estate professional.

Don't forget to check out our Social Media Bootcamp for real estate agents at www.globalrealestateschool.com.

Tip #4: Send Out Introductory Letters

My mother used to say, "Don't hide your light under a bushel." If you want to succeed as a real estate agent, then you need to let people know you are actively working as a real estate professional and open for business.

Sending an introductory letter is an excellent way to let your sphere of influence know about your new career. To help you with this task, I have prepared a sample letter you can download for FREE at globalrealestateschool.com, or go directly to the New Agent Toolkit.

Feel free to edit the letter as you need and also check with your broker to have them help you include any additional information about the company. Your broker might also help with providing stationery, envelopes, and postage. If not, it's still an excellent investment for you to budget for during your first 30 days as a real estate agent.

By the way, there's another good question to ask brokers and managers during your interview. "Would you be willing to cover my postage, stationery, and envelopes for my introductory letters I plan to mail out to my sphere of influence?"

Tip #5: Follow-Up with a Phone Call

Step number five is critical and a must-do to include after you have sent out your introductory letter to your sphere of influence. Follow-up with a phone call!

I have a sample phone call script you might consider on my website. Go to globalrealestateschool.com. Just look under the resources tab and select the New Agent Toolkit, or click here. Feel free to edit the script, but whatever method or style you plan to use, make sure you follow up on your introductory letter with a phone call.

Tip #6: Send Out Letter Number Two

Staying top of mind is important to grow your new real estate business. Yes, you have sent an introductory letter, followed up with a phone call, and now it's time to send out letter number two. Why? Because you have to begin to train your friends, family members, and former coworkers that when they think of real estate, they need to think of you! Without a consistent follow-up system, your friends may forget about you.

With the third form of contact, you are slowly beginning to help them realize you are serious about your new career. When friends think or hear of real estate leads, they will refer to any potential prospects your way.

You can download a sample letter for FREE at globalrealestateschool.com. Just look under the resources tab and select the 'New Agent Toolkit.'

Tip #7: Send Out a Market Statistics Postcard

This type of marketing is extremely easy to produce using your local Multiple Listing Service and the latest statistics from your market area. You can watch a sample webinar by going to www.globalrealestateschool.com. Once there, select the resources tab and then look under the 'New Agent Toolkit.' Look for the link, "Statistics and Your Local Marketplace."

Of course, there are many other marketing ideas to generate business as a new real estate professional. For my complete 101 Marketing Tips to Grow Your Real Estate Sales Career, go to Global Real Estate School and order a copy today!

Conclusion

Thanks for purchasing my tips book, Tips for Successfully Passingthe Real Estate Exam and Generate Income in Your First 90 Days!

I wish you the best of luck on the exam, but more importantly, in your sales career as a new real estate professional. I sincerely hope you enjoy this profession as much as I do.

Always feel free to reach out to me and be sure and tell others looking for a career in real estate to visit www.globalrealestateschool.com.

Best of luck,

John D. Mayfield
The Real Estate Tech Guy
Author | Broker | Keynote Speaker
www.globalrealestateschool.com

ABOUT THE AUTHOR

John Mayfield received his real estate license in 1978 at the age of 18. John has been a practicing broker since 1981 and has owned and operated as many as three offices in Southeast Missouri during his real estate career. John has taught pre and post license real estate courses since 1988. John has earned the ABR®, ABRM, CRB, CIPS, e-PRO®, GRI, RENE, (Real Estate Negotiation Expert) Military and SRS designations throughout his real estate tenure.

John is also a 2015 Graduate from REALTOR® University's Master of Real Estate Program, and recipient of the Capstone Award for his thesis paper. John has earned both REALTOR-Associate and REALTOR of the Year from his local board and received the 2014 Richard A. Mendenhall Leadership award from Missouri REALTORS and the REBI Hall of Leaders Award in San Francisco, CA at the NAR Conference.

John has spoken to thousands of real estate professionals in over 25 countries throughout his speaking career. He is the author of eight books and creator of the "5-Minutes Series for Real Estate Agents," Cengage Learning, with over 25,000 copies sold. He is the co-author of 21 Mistakes Real Estate Brokers Make and How to Avoid Them, Acclaim Press with Corky Hyatt.

John is also active on a local, state and national level for the REALTORS® Association, and served as the 2010 President of the CRB Council of Real Estate Brokers and Managers. John is Liaison for the National Association of REALTORS® to Greece, Serbia and Bulgaria and the Missouri REALTORS 2020 Treasurer.

John has two children, Allie and Anne, and he and his wife Kerry live in Farmington, MO, where John owns and operates a "virtual" real estate firm, an online real estate school, (Global Real Estate School) and speaks full-time around the U.S. and internationally.

Connect with me at:

Instagram - @realestatetechguy

Facebook – GlobalRealEstateSchool

YouTube – GlobalRealEstateSchool

LinkedIn – JohnDMayfield

Twitter - @JohnMayfield

Podcast – www.GlobalRealEstateSchoolPodcast.com

Need help passing the real estate exam? Check out www.MyRealEstateExamCoach.com. Also, follow John at www.BusinessTechGuy.com

John D. Mayfield